SSAT
on
Future
Learning

Alex Galvin

ISBN: 978-0-9930511-7-3

Published August 2017
Editor: Peter Chambers
Design: SSAT Creative

SSAT (The Schools Network) Ltd, Central House, 142 Central Street, London, EC1V 8AR
ssatuk.co.uk

SSAT on Future Learning

FOREWORD

Dr William Rankin, director of Unfold Learning
and worldwide director of learning for Apple 2013-2016

One of the most difficult challenges for many of us in education is the constant pressure to be innovative, try harder, and do better. Certainly, we want to do well by the learners in our classrooms and schools, and many of us try resolutely to keep up with the nearly constant stream of new technologies and approaches that characterise our field. However, the relentless pace of new, more, and better can be exhausting. Indeed, it can tempt some of us just to give up. After all, why should we try new methods or change what we do and how we do it just so that in a week or a month or a year another brand new 'solution' can replace the one we've just worked so hard to integrate into our practice?

The purpose of this document – and of SSAT more broadly – is to give you a map through the confusing jungle of possibilities that distinguishes today's education, to offer the community and guidance of fellow travellers, and to cheer you on your path. Is education changing? Of course. But what's important is how it's changing. The fundamental shift here is not essentially technological; it's a shift in who we are and what we do as teachers. As this document puts it, it's "a shift to thinking of teachers as constructors of learning opportunities rather than transmitters of information." While that may sound unnerving at first, making such a shift can be incredibly rewarding. It can bring the joy and energy of learning back to teaching. And it allows us to see our work – and our learners – in less fragmentary, more holistic ways.

But why should we make this change in the first place? After all, teachers as 'transmitters of information' has a prodigious history. The answer has nothing to do with fads or fashions, but everything to do with a foundational shift in the way information is created and moves. When information had a limited number of controlled and vetted channels to get to our learners, and when we could mostly trust the information that came through those channels, it made sense to emphasise behaviours of informational trust: transmission, absorption, and replication. But today, when information comes through myriad channels, not all of which are trustworthy, we need our learners to be far more discerning. They'll have to have the wisdom to understand which information is real and which isn't and they'll need to practise the skills necessary to discover, assemble, and integrate it in their work. This change means we can no longer focus on transmission. We must design learning experiences where diverse learners can practise all of these skills. How do we do that? Well, since you asked...

Dr William Rankin
Richmond, Virginia
william.rankin@me.com

FUTURE LEARNING: WHAT KIND OF LEARNING FOR WHAT KIND OF FUTURE?

In May 2017 SSAT led future learning seminars around the country with Dr William Rankin, director of Unfold Learning and until recently the worldwide director of learning at Apple. This publication is a culmination of those discussions, our extensive work in the field of curriculum and learning and Dr Rankin's most recent research. This publication aims to capture some of the wisdom shared by our member schools during the workshop and offer further food for thought.

In 1995, Newsweek ran an article entitled *Why the web won't be nirvana*, it stated:

> "Visionaries see a future of telecommuting workers, interactive libraries and multimedia classrooms. They speak of electronic town meetings and virtual communities. Commerce and business will shift from offices and malls to networks and modems. And the freedom of digital networks will make government more democratic. Baloney."
>
> *Clifford Stoll, Newsweek, 1995*

To many of us at the seminars, 1995 doesn't feel all that long ago. But back in 1995, many aspects of our lives today would have sounded like science fiction. The article poured scorn on the suggestion that we would be accessing books and newspapers, shopping, making restaurant reservations and buying airline tickets online.

It is very easy in hindsight to laugh at the misplaced certainty of pieces like this, but of course, few of us would have predicted how technology would transform so many aspects of our lives. In less than 25 years the ways in which we live – how we communicate, how we work and innumerable aspects of our day-to-day life have been fundamentally altered by our relationship with technology. Back in 1995 we were still nine years from the creation of Facebook and Google maps; the iPhone was 12 years away.

And of course, technology has also changed how we learn and how we acquire knowledge. We have immediate access to unimaginable amounts of information at the touch of a button. The answers to almost any questions can probably be found via a small device that most of us have in our pocket at all times. We expect immediate access to highly accurate information – whether it's what time the next bus will arrive, what our medical symptoms might mean or historical facts. We are no longer limited by who we have access to, the books we have within reach or what we can retain in our memories. Arguably the democratisation of learning is now more dependent on access to technology than access to books and other resources.

KNOWLEDGE VS SKILLS DEBATE

This context, combined with the oft-repeated line that we are 'preparing young people for jobs that may not yet exist' has fed into an ongoing 'knowledge vs skills' debate. Does a knowledge-based curriculum lose its relevance if we cannot structure the content to support future employability? If we focus on skills, are we dumbing down and denying our young people access to cultural capital?

However, it surely goes without saying that we do not want young people leaving our schools with empty heads and hands full of technology. Consideration of future learning cannot be about knowledge vs skills. Clearly any attempt to develop skills without also focusing on acquiring and applying knowledge will always be a very hollow exercise. Conversely, mastery of a subject or discipline can never be achieved by retaining information alone. We want our young people to develop a love of learning, not just to see it as a means to an end. We want our young people to become knowledgeable, well-informed, culturally engaged adults who can navigate all of the complexities of the world we live in.

Access to information is not the same as knowing and understanding. In our world of 'fake news', where social media feeds us a diet of information that reinforces our views, it has surely never been more important for our young people to be able to apply accurate knowledge to what they hear and read. Our young people need to be able to question the 'truths' they are presented with, to make sound moral and ethical judgements and to challenge inequalities. We want our students to be able to critically evaluate information – to be able to use their knowledge to check the logic of what they are hearing and to think deeply about the information to which they have access. The DIKW pyramid, which explores the relationship between information and knowledge, reinforces that our learners need more than data and information, we need to support them in moving towards knowledge and wisdom.

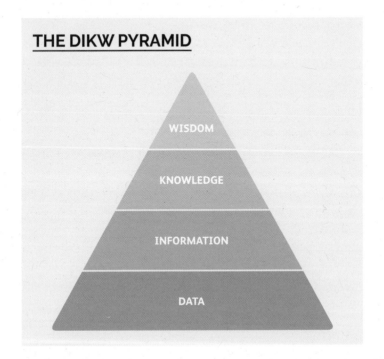

THE DIKW PYRAMID

WISDOM

KNOWLEDGE

INFORMATION

DATA

Teachers and schools have a central role to play in enabling young people to acquire knowledge and wisdom. Having immediate access to information is not the same as learning. Developing educated, well-rounded young people depends on far more than being able to find the answers to things. While the technology exists for learning to take place virtually, and on occasions this may be extremely helpful, there is little appetite for this to become the default approach. The interactions that school provides, the way in which skilled teachers structure learning

Clearly any attempt to develop skills without also focusing on acquiring and applying knowledge will always be a very hollow exercise

opportunities to inspire and motivate, and the opportunities that a broad and balanced curriculum offer all play a crucial role in the holistic development of young people. The wider curriculum and the experience of being part of a community provide opportunities for prosocial modelling and play a significant role in the positive development of young people.

However, to focus exclusively on knowledge acquisition also does our young people a disservice. We don't need to be able to see the future to know that they will need more than factual knowledge to be successful and to develop as well-rounded individuals. All students deserve access to a curriculum that challenges and inspires them, supporting them both in acquiring knowledge and developing as an individual. Many of the best schools are already ensuring that their students access a broad and balanced academic curriculum whilst also providing opportunities to develop the skills they will need for future success.

WHAT SKILLS DO OUR YOUNG PEOPLE NEED FOR THE FUTURE?

Let's assume that we don't know quite what the future holds for our young people. Some may find themselves doing jobs that we can't yet imagine, many will end up doing jobs that are entirely or at least partially familiar to us all. What we do know, is that irrespective of job descriptions, society continues to change at a rapid rate and the way that we work and live will change accordingly.

In 2014 the UK Commission for Employment and Skills published *The Future of Work: Jobs and Skills in 2030*. This report identified six key trends (notes in brackets are our words, not from the original report):

1. **Technological growth and expansion** (the impact of technology on employment and skills will continue to expand, across most sectors).
2. **Interconnectivity and collaboration** (work will be more interconnected and employees will need to be skilled collaborators. This will include virtual collaboration and it may be that fewer people are office-based).

3. **Convergence of innovation** (innovation will increasingly occur through people working across different sectors and disciplines).
4. **Increased individual responsibility** (employees will increasingly be expected to take responsibility for their own skills development and personal brand).
5. **The shrinking middle** (the number of jobs available for employees in the middle of the skills hierarchy will decline at a rapid rate.).
6. **The four-generational workplace** (the workplace of the future will often have different generations working side by side. Traditional ideas about hierarchy and seniority will become less important).

This, and other research such as *The Future of Jobs, Employment, Skills and Workforce Strategy for the Fourth Industrial Revolution*, published by the World Economic Forum draw similar conclusions. With technology driving increased automation, there will be lower demand for routine manual labour. Some of our young people will be at the forefront of technological innovation in the future, but even for those who aren't there are clear messages about the skills and attributes that they will need.

"Overall, social skills – such as persuasion, emotional intelligence and teaching others – will be in higher demand across industries than narrow technical skills, such as programming or equipment operation and control. In essence, technical skills will need to be supplemented with strong social and collaboration skills."

The Future of Jobs, Employment, Skills and Workforce Strategy for the Fourth Industrial Revolution, World Economic Forum

Drawing from our work with SSAT member schools as well as previous research, we can make some informed suggestions about the attributes our students are likely to need.

7 key skills and qualities for future success

Lifelong learning and personal responsibility for skills development.
Technology continues to drive rapid change in the way that most jobs operate. As a result, successful employees will need to keep refreshing their knowledge and skills and will need to take responsibility for their own professional development.

Self-motivation and flexibility.
As increasing numbers of people work remotely and the free-lance economy expands significantly, employees will need high levels of self-discipline, the ability to organise their own time and flexibility to work across a rapidly changing work environment.

Effective communication skills.
The ability to communicate clearly verbally and in writing and to influence the thinking of others remains as important as ever. Remote working adds a new dimension to this – the need to be able to communicate effectively and appropriately via technology, often working with people who are in a different location, very possibly in another country.

Ability to transfer knowledge and skills.
Innovation will be driven across different sectors and people are more likely to have a number of careers during their working life. As a result, the ability to apply knowledge and skills

in different contexts, recognising links and synergies, will be invaluable. Employees will need to be able to move between different sectors, showing that they are agile and resilient.

Ability to work collaboratively.
Employees will need to be able to work collaboratively, with colleagues of different generations and in different locations who they rarely meet in person. The ability to work with others to find innovative solutions to problems will become ever more important.

Creativity and problem solving.
As the number of cognitive and routine manual jobs stagnate, non-routine manual and cognitive jobs will continue to increase. People who can demonstrate the ability to think differently to solve problems and those who can work effectively with others to innovate will be in high demand.

Analytical skills.
In an age where there is almost limitless access to data, the ability to analyse information, formulate and test hypotheses and to think independently will be key. A strong foundation of core knowledge and disciplinary skills is needed to do this successfully.

So where does this leave us as educators? To reiterate again, consideration of the kind of skills our young people will need is not about rejecting the importance of knowledge acquisition. Learning is not only about creating employable young people and we should not need to justify curriculum choices or approaches to learning on the basis that they will have a direct relevance to the jobs that young people will have in the future. We want young people to appreciate the innate value of learning something new and gaining a broader understanding of the world. We also want to ensure that all students have access to 'the best that has been thought and said' in all cultures and traditions – learning that develops their cultural capital and enables them to think. And it is worth acknowledging that successful schools have always found ways to develop knowledge and skills, irrespective of the emphasis being placed by government or current trends in thinking.

We also need to recognise that schools can't do everything, particularly at a time of significantly restricted budgets and recruitment challenges. On this basis, a realistic consideration of future learning needs to start from the assumption that this is not about throwing everything up in the air and starting again. Neither is it about substantial investment in technology. We need to find ways to support young people in developing the skills they need within current realities and find answers that support teachers rather than adding to the pressure placed on them.

So, the question is, how can we make space for more...

Creativity?

Student-led learning?

Collaboration?

Practice spaces?

Failure?

Real-world learning?

Connectivity?

Making?

Opportunities for the student to act as curator/selector?

Social learning?

THE ROLE OF CURRICULUM

"The real curriculum is the lived daily experience of young people in classrooms... curriculum is pedagogy."

Dylan Wiliam, Redesigning Schooling 3: Principled curriculum design

Recent years have brought such extensive changes to curriculum at all key stages that curriculum can easily be conflated with qualifications and accountability. It is hard to keep a broader perspective when grappling with ever-changing expectations. We know that Ofsted are concerned about a narrowing of the curriculum offer and a lack of clarity about curriculum intent in some schools. This focus reflects wider concerns that stringent accountability measures combined with funding pressures have led some schools to restrict their curriculum offer – with content being driven almost entirely by GCSE specifications or concerns about school performance measures.

SSAT has long-championed a principled approach to curriculum design, through our work on personalisation with David Hargreaves, and more recently with Dylan Wiliam through *Redesigning Schooling*. School-led principled curriculum design is core to discussion of future learning.

In considering the role of curriculum in future learning then, we must be clear about what we mean by the term. It is helpful to draw a distinction between three things: the national curriculum – the learning that is prescribed by the government; the school curriculum – the programme of study determined by the school or academy; and the real curriculum – the reality of what students actually experience, which is always created by teachers.

Here, we are primarily concerned with the latter two. When we talk about curriculum in this context, we are thinking in the terms outlined by Dylan Wiliam above – *the lived daily experience*. And this goes beyond schools. The way in which young people respond to the school curriculum is shaped to a significant extent by their lived daily experience outside the school. When we think about curriculum as the entirety of young peoples' experiences, new opportunities present themselves. In every school, the curriculum is much more than the collection of GCSEs students leave with. Their experience is hugely dependent on pedagogy, as Dylan Wiliam flags (more on that in the next section), but it is also dependent on the quality of the core curriculum content, plus the wider experiences that are provided within and beyond the classroom.

Approaches such as the National Baccalaureate, which is supported by SSAT, explore wider curriculum models which recognise learning in its widest sense. For instance, schools piloting the National Baccalaureate are offering structured opportunities for an independent project, links with local employers and education providers and recognising wider learning, be it through sport, community involvement or student leadership activities. This in no way downgrades the importance of students' core learning (the work they are doing in subjects), but it recognises that wider learning is important too.

Looking at the curriculum in its widest sense offers a mechanism for ensuring breadth and depth. It can provide experiences for students which enable them to gain the skills mentioned in the previous section – clearly the best way to develop skills is to practise them. Opportunities for students to analyse real world problems, to take the lead in planning an activity, or to structure their own learning are invaluable – not only because they support future employability but also because they enable learning experiences that can be motivating and hugely rewarding.

I recently met a student at Farlingaye High School, who was part of a team that were the national award winner of the CISCO Little Big Awards. The project asked them to "Connect the unconnected" and design something that could be connected usefully to the internet. Their invention was a mouse-trap which could tweet the owner to let them know when it had caught a mouse. The student was rightly bursting with pride and excitement about their achievement. There is no doubt that the project provided invaluable experiences – innovating, planning, making, pitching an idea, working within a team. But it was much more than that.

We can plan for memorable learning experiences, opportunities to innovate, make and do, without suggesting that learning, and curriculum decisions should all be determined by their potential usefulness for future careers. However, what is important is to ensure that these opportunities are not left to chance, or are only accessed by a few highly motivated students. Inventive use of curriculum time – one-off days, themed weeks or longer-term projects – can provide an opportunity for young people to immerse themselves in learning, try new ideas, problem solve and create.

Four pillars of principled curriculum design

A focus on curriculum intent can be extremely useful in considering provision in its widest sense. SSAT's 'Four pillars of principled curriculum design' (available free of charge to SSAT members) supports schools in reviewing how decisions about curriculum are made. The four pillars (Intent, Content, Delivery and Experience) move from focusing on what you want to be distinctive about your offer, through how this informs decisions about content, to how your intent is realised in pedagogy and practice and what impact it has on your students.

This kind of mapping can be very helpful in terms of considering the different ways in which your curriculum supports your students' future success, in the broadest sense. The best curriculum models offer rich learning experiences, both in and out of the classroom, which fire enthusiasm, enable students to discover and pursue new interests, and develop skills that will support them in later life while maintaining a secure academic base.

Learning that encourages students to work more autonomously supports knowledge acquisition while also developing wider skills for life beyond school

None of this requires a radical reimagining of your curriculum. It might involve a clearer articulation of your curriculum intent and a tightening of provision beyond the classroom to ensure that all students receive their full entitlement. It does not require a watering down of curriculum content or a focus on skills at the expense of academic rigour. Learning that encourages students to work more autonomously supports knowledge acquisition, while also developing wider skills for life beyond school.

The kind of skills previously discussed can be developed and embedded through a blend of regular timetabled lessons and structured broader learning opportunities. It does not require additional financial investment or the need to fit new programmes of study into the curriculum. It is more a question of being clear about the kind of learning that will support young people in developing the skills that they require and embedding that into whatever curriculum model works best for you and your context. Learning that encourages students to work more autonomously supports knowledge acquisition while also developing wider skills for life beyond school.

BRINGING FUTURE LEARNING INTO THE CLASSROOM

Before we go any further, it is important to say that the kind of learning that will support young people in the workplaces of the future is already very evident in many classrooms up and down the country. Skilled teachers are well used to bringing the best out of the young people that they work with. Clearly positive relationships, ethos and culture are key to supporting learning. The shifts required to support the development of the skills that have been discussed are subtle ones, not a rejection of commonly shared ideas about good teaching and learning. It is not about completely changing how things are done all of the time, but about thinking where there might be opportunities to reposition the dynamic between teacher and student in order to give students the autonomy to structure their own learning.

"Learning experiences are active, personal, collaborative and relevant, designed to empower learners to be creators who believe their work matters."

Innovation in Schools, Apple (2017)

We need our young people to be able to learn independently, to synthesise, analyse and solve problems. To achieve this, we need to put the focus on the student, enabling them to navigate their own learning, providing genuinely challenging tasks that allow for learning in less controlled environments. Our natural instinct as teachers is often to simplify, to break up learning into manageable chunks, to structure and to scaffold. And, in certain circumstances that might be entirely appropriate. However, we also need to make space to ask bigger questions such as:

- "What happens if...?"
- "Our end point is X, how do we get there?"
- "What do we need to find out?"
- "How can we make sense of this?"
- "How could we improve...?"

Making space for students to create, connect ideas and collaborate is not about a rejection of the importance of knowledge – rather, knowledge is a prerequisite for accessing higher levels of learning. Memorable learning experiences support knowledge acquisition. Over time and with practice, students become increasingly autonomous in their learning. They move from being highly dependent on the structures provided by the teacher to being able to sequence their own learning, selecting and curating from the available data and making well-reasoned decisions. As William Rankin puts it, it is about providing "chances for exploration and application and to exercise and demonstrate how wise practitioners evaluate both opportunities and products within a discipline". It is a shift to thinking of teachers as constructors of learning opportunities rather than transmitters of information.

SSAT talks about this in terms of nurturing 'effective learner behaviours'. In other words, supporting the development of the multi-faceted personal and social skills that enable someone to become an effective learner. Young people need to become increasingly autonomous, not only learning how to use different strategies but also monitoring and reviewing their learning to determine which strategies have been most effective. Through direct involvement in metacognitive processes, they become increasingly confident in structuring their own learning, establishing behaviours that will support them far beyond school. There are many different ways of approaching this; but the best pedagogical models are strategically planned while flexible. Young people need to become increasingly autonomous, learning how to use different strategies and monitoring/reviewing their learning to see which strategies have been most effective. In considering this, we believe it is useful to distinguish between what effective learners are, and what they can do (see opposite).

Young people need to become increasingly autonomous, learning how to use different strategies and monitoring/reviewing their learning to see which strategies have been most effective

Effective learning behaviours need to be carefully fostered within the classroom. This requires a focus at whole-school level on the development and modelling of effective teacher behaviours as well as students' learning behaviours. Over time students and teachers become more self-aware and able to articulate learning processes. Teachers need to be able to

SSAT believes effective learners are:

- responsible
- critical thinkers and problem solvers
- engaged in the learning process
- resilient and persistent (shows grit) – flexible/adaptable
- creative and creating
- curious and questioning
- knowledgeable and confident
- good communicators and team players
- digitally literate
- aspirational.

Effective learners can:

- seek relevance and make links to beliefs and experiences
- anticipate, reflect, analyse, justify and plan ahead
- develop a toolkit of strategies to learn
- have the attributes to be work and world ready (content and learning process)
- inquire and innovate
- achieve
- challenge the accepted wisdom
- collaborate with others
- motivate themselves and others to achieve.

model effective learning behaviours before expecting to see them in their students.

Rather than talking about 'independent learning' therefore, it may be more helpful to think about developing independent learners – independent thinkers, people who can make informed choices and will continue to be effective learners once the support structures of school are removed. While some students are naturally effective independent learners, many are not, and need careful guidance over time to gain the confidence and self-awareness required. Research such as Carol Dweck's *Mindset* and *The 16 Habits of Mind*, developed by Prof Art Costa and Dr Bena Kallick, reinforce the idea that we need to support our students to develop as positive, curious learners, confident in their abilities to gain more knowledge and master new skills. We want young people who leave school with the ability to think flexibly and creatively about a problem.

A consideration of exploratory talk (Mercer and Littleton, 2007) may also be useful here. A key step towards students driving their own learning is developing the ability to work effectively and efficiently with others. Deliberately modelling and structuring discussion which encourages students to share emerging ideas, collaboratively explore different perspectives and seek consensus helps students to shape their own ideas and recognise the value of their personal contribution to the learning process.

Developing independent learners takes time. It doesn't mean that all learning should be student-led, or that students should be expected to demonstrate independent learning skills straight away. It is a process through which students take increasing responsibility for their own development. Counter-intuitively, the journey to independent learning is not always made through learning independently. It is about an ongoing conversation about learning – about the choices that students make and the impact that those choices have. It is about over time, empowering students to make their own decisions about how they learn and how they tackle a challenge.

William Rankin's 'cubic learning model' provides a useful mechanism for exploring this. He divides learning into three facets: content, community and context.

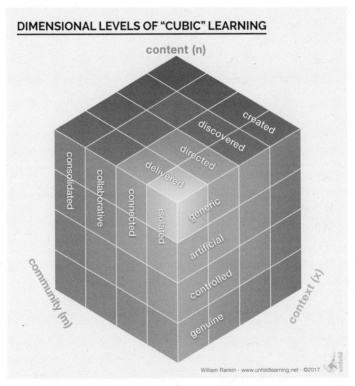

DIMENSIONAL LEVELS OF "CUBIC" LEARNING

content (n)

created
discovered
directed
delivered
generic
artificial
controlled
genuine

consolidated
collaborative
connected
isolated

community (m)

context (x)

William Rankin · www.unfoldlearning.net · ©2017

Each facet provides a taxonomy through which learning opportunities can be reviewed. Clearly, this is not to suggest that all learning opportunities should have students operating at the highest levels all of the time – there will be occasions where it is entirely valid to be operating at the lower levels in some or indeed all three facets. However, it is important to consider where there might be opportunities to enable students to access the higher levels.

DIMENSIONS OF CONTENT

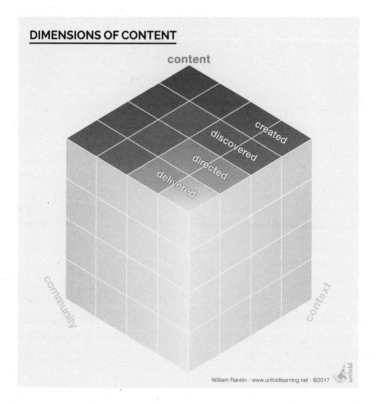

William Rankin · www.unfoldlearning.net · ©2017

A focus on content moves from direct delivery from teacher to student, through increasing degrees of autonomy, to the highest level where the student is creating their own material. Content is pivotal within the cube model, recognising that a level of knowledge is required to access the community and context dimensions fully.

At its highest level, the learner is moving into expert territory, building on existing content and creating outputs that contribute something new to the discipline – a new hypothesis or way of synthesising existing knowledge. Or they might be making something new, drawing on the previous stages of development and supporting the learning of others. This is the kind of learning we would expect to see at the highest levels of academic study, but it is also accessible by the youngest and most inexperienced of learners, given the right opportunities. For example, a student might design and create video content which provides a personal, unique way of communicating content. Through the opportunity to create, they have been able to make the discipline their own and replay content in a way that supports the learning of others.

At the highest level of content, the learner is making something new, drawing on previous stages of development and supporting others' learning

This kind of sophisticated understanding of content has been given a greater focus in the reformed national curriculum and through assessments at key stage 2, 4 and 5. Students need to be able to engage with content at a deep level to demonstrate true understanding. At the highest level of content, the learner is making something new, drawing on previous stages of development and supporting others' learning. This is the kind of autonomy our learners need to work towards in order to demonstrate a deep engagement with content:

> "As learners, our need for delivery diminishes as we develop more mature relationships with content – as we move deeper into its dimensionality. And moving deeper is the way we engage with and serve a content area as both learners and practitioners. For content truly to be 'king' we must engage with it at levels far deeper than mere reception and we therefore need teaching and learning practices that support our exploration and experience of those deeper levels."
>
> *Dr William Rankin*

DIMENSIONS OF COMMUNITY

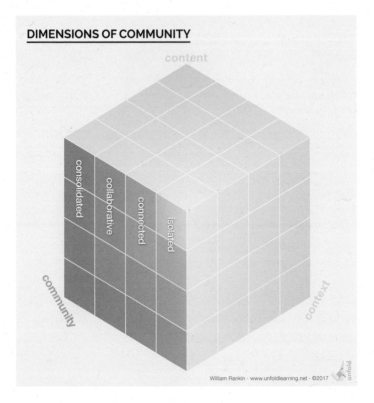

William Rankin · www.unfoldlearning.net · ©2017

In the community dimension, students are moving from working in isolation to working in *truly integrated groups* – to the point that the structure of the group is essential to the success of the project. At this level, learners are required to demonstrate high level skills – determining strategy and methodology as well as interpersonal skills. Research such as that by Phil Schlechty has suggested that it tends to be through this kind of collaborative work that people are empowered to perform at their highest level. The sense of collective responsibility and need to find solutions drives people to learn more; motivating them to strive to achieve and feel a greater sense of personal achievement when things work well.

That is not to say that all learning should focus on opportunities to work in groups. Clearly, there are times when there is a need for personal reflection; opportunities to focus, absorb information and think through problems. Different kinds of learning all have their place and as young people become more skilled and self-aware as learners they should increasingly be able to determine the right learning approaches for particular tasks. However, it is essential that learners recognise and understand the importance of working collaboratively. Even work that has been produced in isolation will benefit from being brought in front of a community – for review, feedback, discussion and further development. Building this community aspect of learning reinforces the ways in which students support each other's development, and provides powerful ways of making learning more meaningful. Working for the benefit of a group, or preparing something to present to an audience, will always be more motivational than producing an assignment that has no life beyond its submission.

At the highest level of community, the group's structure is essential to the project's success and people are empowered to perform at their best

Work experience can also provide invaluable opportunities for students to contribute to a team and work alongside colleagues outside their age range. At the highest level of community, the group's structure is essential to the project's success and people are empowered to perform at their best.

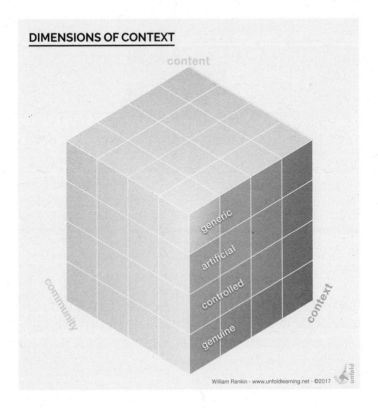

DIMENSIONS OF CONTEXT

content

generic

artificial

controlled

genuine

community

context

William Rankin · www.unfoldlearning.net · ©2017

Context is a vitally important and complex element of learners' experience. It can refer to the physical environment in which students are operating, but also refers to the other factors which influence the ways in which learning takes place – prior experience, the wider social, economic, historical and political context in which we operate – local, national and international. And of course, much of what is studied in schools has a contextual element. We create case studies and examples to support young people in making connections and seeing relevance.

In the context dimension, students move from situations which are entirely generic, working in environments that are not truly connected to the learning that is happening, to experiences in which they are immersed in a genuine context. When operating at the highest level, students engage fully with the context, interrogate it and adapt their methodology accordingly. This genuine context opens students up to risk – to the possibility of failure and the responsibility of finding a solution that works. As such, it is enabling students to face the kind of situations that they might face in the real world, ones in which they are truly accountable for the success of the project and in which they are dealing with real problems without predetermined answers.

It is not always easy to see how these kinds of opportunities might fit within the curriculum, given the need to cover all specified content. It can also feel uncomfortable for the teacher since it requires control of the task to move to the student. Teachers need to be accept that the progression of the work may

Opportunities to undertake real projects provide invaluable, memorable learning experiences and insights which cannot be accessed by simulated and controlled tasks

take learners in unpredictable directions. At times, they may hit a brick wall and be unable to progress any further. So teachers need to work alongside their students, as a member of a 'community of practice' rather than structuring the learning. However, the opportunity to engage with the real world and undertake real projects provide invaluable, memorable learning experiences and insights which cannot be accessed by simulated and controlled tasks. These kinds of projects can also offer challenge of a different kind – and as such the rewards that come with finding a solution, persevering when you are stuck and seeing a longer-term project through to fruition. Opportunities to undertake real projects in this way provide invaluable, memorable learning experiences and insights which cannot be accessed by simulated and controlled tasks.

THE ROLE OF TECHNOLOGY

Discussion of future learning often leads quickly into a consideration of the role that technology could or should play. We know that our students, like us, will reach for their phones when they want to find out information. We also know that technology will play a key role in the work lives of the vast majority of our students – regardless of the line of employment they choose.

However, this does not mean that technology has all of the answers when it comes to future learning. Most importantly it is essential that we are clear about what we want to achieve with technology – how it can enhance what we are doing and how it is supporting the development of our young people. The SAMR model, produced by Dr Rueben Puentedura talks about this as the move from technology as a means of enhancing learning to the point where it is transforming learning, or from 'substitution' to 'redefinition'.

Apple talk about three stages of innovation in learning through technology:
- Introducing
- Integrating
- Innovating.

We need to consider whether technology is truly changing learning or whether it is just acting as a replacement for another way of doing things. However, we should not dismiss the ways in which technology may offer functional improvements to learning as unimportant. Technology use does not need to be redefining learning to be valuable. The key here is to be clear about how and why technology is being used and also to ensure that there are some opportunities for students to innovate through technology.

Certainly, to use the terminology of William Rankin's cube model, technology can offer exciting routes into learning which is 'created', 'consolidated' and 'genuine'. However, it is important not to view this as a hierarchy, which only sees highly innovative teaching through technology as worthwhile. There will be very valid reasons for using technology in a wide range of ways. The technology is not the key focus here, teaching and learning must always take priority. As John Hattie puts it:

> "Going all out to power new teaching innovations with technology (not the other way around)."

Visible Learning for Teachers: Maximizing Impact on Learning
John Hattie, 2012

Some of the most exciting opportunities that are unlocked through technology come when students are leading their own learning. Once students are using technology to create, to innovate or to shape their own learning, it is offering opportunities which might not otherwise be available. It is interesting that Apple's model puts the emphasis firmly on the student's use of technology, not the teacher's. The teacher's role here is to structure learning experiences and to create an environment which motivates and supports students.

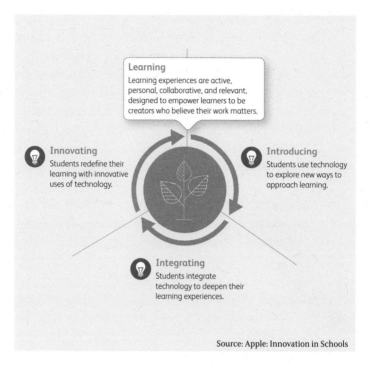

Source: Apple: Innovation in Schools

The role that technology can play in future learning goes far beyond educating young people in using equipment. We might summarise the different roles that technology can play as follows:

- Computational thinking
- Inspiration and motivation
- Supporting independent learning
- Protocols and security.

Computational thinking

Learning about and with technology can play a key role in developing students' skills. Computational thinking supports the development of critical thinking skills, supporting students in structuring, sequencing and spotting patterns – skills that can be developed with or without the direct use of technological equipment. In order to achieve high levels of competency in use of technology, students need to be extremely competent at problem-solving – at deconstructing a problem, identifying what should and could be done and devising a process. It requires students to identify and test hypotheses, to explore and to create. As Miles Berry puts it:

> "We want students to look for faster, simpler, more elegant solutions to the same problem, avoiding unnecessary repetition or using automation to speed up common tasks."
>
> *http://milesberry.net/2017/02*
> *computational-thinking-and-technology/*

Activities which develop young people's skills in technology, for example in coding, often also have far wider implications for their skills development. The skills that computational thinking particularly supports – creating, collaborating, problem-solving – have clear relevance to any consideration of future learning. The experience of repeating, refining and modifying processes teaches important lessons about continuous improvement, and about resilience. It is not difficult to see the parallels between the skills of computational thinking, effective learner behaviours and William Rankin's cube model.

Inspiration and motivation
When used well, technology can create a sense of wonder, opening doors and firing students' imagination. Whereas once we might have been reliant on a line drawing to explain the workings of the heart, today, students can access interactive tools that enable them to explore for themselves. Virtual

reality (VR) equipment enables students to see animations floating in front of them or to explore the surface of Mars. The ability to model in 3D can enable students who struggle with spatial awareness to access higher level problems. With low-cost cardboard headsets now available, more and more schools are experimenting with VR in the classroom.

Even without VR equipment, technology offers boundless opportunities for students to explore and create. One of the most frequent comments from schools that have introduced iPads/tablets or who are encouraging students to use their own devices in class is that the students immediately find ways to use them to support their learning that the teachers hadn't foreseen. Technology can also have a significant impact on learning opportunities for students with a learning or physical disability – as has been seen in much innovative practice in special schools.

Supporting independent learning

This kind of learning, learning which encourages exploration and creation, also supports young people in working independently. Technology can also provide the kind of real-world contexts that have been previously discussed as well as enabling collaboration locally, nationally and internationally. It can support more substantial collaborative projects, enabling groups to continue to develop their ideas beyond the constraints of lesson time and the school day.

Technology also enables independent learning beyond school hours – offering students the opportunity to access resources and links as well as the potential to connect with each other and feed back on each other's work. Requiring students to submit work, collaborate, comment on each other's assignments and interact with the teacher all provide useful experience of the kinds of online environments they are likely to be working with beyond school. Opportunities to learn independently through technology can also provide new routes to learning for students with a disability, or those whose family circumstances may limit their ability to engage with certain aspects of school life.

Protocols and security

As already discussed, students' confidence in using technology doesn't negate the need for support and education. Students need the skills to be able to interrogate the information that they can access online – to navigate the enormous amount of content available and to make informed judgements about what they read. They need to leave schools as smart consumers of technology – fully cognisant of the opportunities and limitations of the technology that they are using. They need careful guidance about personal safety online and the inherent risks of social media use.

Technology can also play an important role in supporting the softer skills and attributes that young people will need in the future, be that in the workplace or further study. Many schools now operate systems through which students work collaboratively online – enabling them to work with students remotely, in different classes, schools and overseas. The experience of sharing work, peer reviewing and collaborating to develop ideas develops independence. The discipline of uploading work to meet deadlines and using technology to support effective planning and time management all offer useful practice for the kind of activities they may have to manage confidently beyond school.

RECOMMENDATIONS

There are clear parallels between the different constructs for learning development explored in this publication. Whether you are focusing on SSAT's Effective Learning Behaviours (TEEP) or talking about the point at which learning is 'created', 'consolidated' and 'genuine' in William Rankin's cube model, we are working towards common goals.

Future learning is not about a futuristic, unrecognisable model of learning. Nor is it about changing how things are done all of the time or negating the importance of knowledge acquisition. However, to disregard the importance of the kind of skills we have been discussing is to do our young people a disservice. We need to find space to allow our students to explore, create and experience real-world learning. And in doing so, we can create more memorable learning experiences that will support knowledge and understanding.

So, how can we make this work in practice?

12 key recommendations for future learning

1 Revisit your curriculum intent. Ensure that you are clear about what you are trying to achieve with your curriculum and that the vision is shared across the school community.

2 Assess your curriculum provision in terms of the *entirety of students' experiences*. What opportunities does your wider curriculum offer to develop key skills? How many students access them?

3 Provide space for students to practise skills – and to fail. Focus on creating a culture which recognises that mastery takes time and that failure is part of the journey.

4 Ensure that students have the opportunity to structure their own learning – to explore, create and work out how to reach the end goal. This can be done in small ways day-to-day in lessons as well as through long-term collaborative projects. Use curriculum time creatively to give students opportunities to immerse themselves in collaborative projects.

5 Promote talk which is exploratory, tentative and hypothetical. Encourage students to see learning as a collaborative process, in which they can learn from each other and work together to develop ideas.

6 Talk regularly and openly about what it means to be an effective learner. Focus on the progression to being an independent learner and encourage young people to recognise their progress towards being an effective life-long learner.

7   Find opportunities for student-led enquiry and curation. Discuss selection of material and the relative importance of pieces of information for the enquiry.

8   Encourage active learning techniques – intellectually challenging approaches that counter passivity and ensure that all members of the class are engaged.

9   Allow time for students to reflect on their own learning, to identify what helped them to progress and what hindered them. Highlight the importance in using past mistakes to support future progress.

10 Try to find opportunities for real-world learning – this might be through links with the local community or employers, work experience, engaging with national competitions or just through bringing genuine problems into the classroom or student leadership roles in school.

11 Harness the opportunities that technology offers to link into the world beyond the school – to motivate, inspire and provide opportunities for collaboration.

12 Use technology as a tool to support creativity and invention. Allow students to experiment, explore and innovate.

REFERENCES AND FURTHER READING

SSAT
Personalising learning series, David Hargreaves (2006)
ssatuk.co.uk/the-exchange/library/personalising-learning

Redesigning Schooling 2, What kind of teaching for what kind of learning?
Guy Claxton and Bill Lucas, 2013
ssatuk.co.uk/the-exchange/library/redesigning-schooling

Redesigning Schooling 3, Principled curriculum design, Dylan Wiliam, 2013
ssatuk.co.uk/the-exchange/library/redesigning-schooling

Teacher Effectiveness Enhancement Programme (TEEP)
ssatuk.co.uk/teep

Four pillars of principled curriculum design
ssatuk.co.uk/the-exchange/library

Apple Education
Innovation in Schools. Designing learning, teaching and your school environment with Apple, 2017
https://itunes.apple.com/gb/book/innovation-in-schools/id1259499861?mt=11

Research for Educators, 2016
https://itunes.apple.com/gb/book/research-for-educators/id1088992950?mt=11

Dr William Rankin
Unfold Learning
unfoldlearning.net

Links to cubic learning
unfoldlearning.net/links-resources
unfoldlearning.net/2017/05/17/dimensions-of-cubic-learning-content
unfoldlearning.net/2017/05/19/dimensions-of-cubic-learning-community
unfoldlearning.net/2017/05/24/dimensions-of-cubic-learning-context

Miscellaneous

Computational Thinking and Technology blog post (2017), Miles Berry

Dialogue and the Development of Children's Thinking: a sociocultural approach (2007) Mercer, N and Littleton, K.

DIKW pyramid – further information
https://en.wikipedia.org/wiki/DIKW_pyramid

Engaging Students: The Next Level of Working on the Work (2011), Phillip C. Schlechty

Learning and Leading with Habits of Mind: 16 Essential Characteristics for Success (2008), Arthur L. Costa and Bena Kallick

Interthinking: putting talk to work (2013) Littleton,K and Mercer, N.

Mindset: Changing The Way You Think To Fulfil Your Potential (2012), Carol Dweck

National Baccalaureate Trust
http://www.natbacctrust.org/

SAMR model – presentation slides
www.hippasus.com/rrpweblog/archives/2014/11/13/SAMR_FirstSteps.pdf

The Future of Jobs. Employment, Skills and Workforce Strategy for the Fourth Industrial Revolution, 2016, World Economic Forum
http://reports.weforum.org/future-of-jobs-2016/

The future of work: jobs and skills in 2030, UK Commission for Employment and Skills, 2014
https://www.gov.uk/government/publications/jobs-and-skills-in-2030

Visible Learning for Teachers: Maximising Impact on Learning (2012), John Hattie

Why the web won't be nirvana, Clifford Stoll, Newsweek, 1995
http://www.newsweek.com/clifford-stoll-why-web-wont-be-nirvana-185306

Working on the Work: An Action Plan for Teachers, Principals and Superintendents, Phillip C. Schlechty